D1475474

SPORT IMAGES, 2514 SAN PABLO AVENUE, BERKELEY, CALIFORNIA 94702 USA
TELEPHONE: 510–665–9105   FAX: 510–665–9536
COPYRIGHT ©1998 BY UDO MACHAT

ALL RIGHTS RESERVED INCLUDING THE RIGHT OF REPRODUCTION IN WHOLE OR IN PART IN ANY FORM
PRINTED IN HONG KONG

ISBN 0-9618712-4-5

POPPY HILLS GOLF COURSE

PEBBLE BEACH, CALIFORNIA

A SPORT IMAGES BOOK

by Udo Machat

Foreword by Robert Trent Jones, Jr.

SPORT IMAGES, BERKELEY, CALIFORNIA, USA

CONTENTS

FOREWORD

*T*he creation of Poppy Hills Golf Course was the culmination of tremendous vision by the Northern California Golf Association to construct a championship, tournament golf facility for their members and guests. When I first walked the site, it became apparent that Poppy would become something special. It also became obvious that the course would be a challenge to design and build.

Not just because its neighbors included the likes of Cypress Point Club, Pebble Beach Golf Links and Spyglass Hill, but because of the steeply forested terrain and numerous environmental restrictions. On paper, 166 acres sounds like plenty of land. But during the preparation of various routings for the golf course during the initial stages of design, we realized much of the property would be unusable in order to preserve the riparian corridor and Dwarf Cypress trees. Fortunately, we were able to acquire an additional twelve acres from the Pebble Beach Company. Not only did this give us more flexibility, it also reduced earthmoving to an absolute

minimum which was essential for project approval. Additionally, through careful compilation of the topsoil on site, and technical control over the irrigation, we produced a first class golf course within strict budgetary guidelines.

From the outset, my goal was to design a course that would test golfers mentally and physically. Since we knew it would be used for important regional, NCGA and amateur tournaments, we took painstaking effort to devise a variety of holes and strategies, sure to challenge every skill level and every club in the bag.

For instance, although the course plays to a standard 36–36—72, the back nine features three par threes, and three par fives, which is fairly unique. There are many risk-and-reward holes, where aggressive play can result in birdies or double bogeys, depending on your execution. It's a thinker's golf course, and the golfer must be able to execute a variety of shotmaking requirements. I have often compared a golf course to a symphony. Great courses have ebbs and flows, keeping you off balance until the final crescendo. Through the use of doglegs and elevation changes, the flow at Poppy Hills never allows you to relax, keeps you uncomfortable, making it difficult to attain rhythm. If you force shots or lose your concentration, disaster can occur. Conversely, if you stay patient, keep the ball in play and don't get ahead of yourself, you can emerge victorious over its many challenges.

Like all courses, Poppy Hills is a work in progress. The directors and management staff of the Poppy Holding Inc. continue to make improvements, enhancing what I believe to be a splendid addition to the golfing capital of the world. It is my hope that you enjoy reading about the history and background of Poppy Hills as much as we enjoyed in helping to create it.

Robert Trent Jones, Jr.

Palo Alto, California

August 1998

INTRODUCTION

*T*he very first memory I have of golf is when I worked in a design studio in Toronto during the early 70s. A fellow worker named Patrick Nelson had just arrived from London, and had immediately joined a golf club. There was one other fellow in the studio, Al Elliott, who played "the game." The two seemed to be forever locked in a discussion about golf. They mostly talked very low, almost as if there were secrets to be kept. Some of the staff, including myself, played on ice hockey teams and most of "the boys" had been on high school football teams; in other words, this was a macho crowd. Golf, well, they better not talk too loud about this so-called sport. The needling started, all in good fun, ebbing back and forth, until finally Patrick threw down the gauntlet. "Why don't you try it sometime, Udo? It really isn't as easy as you think." I agreed and a few weeks later, on a crisp fall day with a loaner set that surely must have had slick, greasy grips, I found myself on a golf course, having never had a lesson. Pat surely must have been delighted in my naïveté. There isn't very much about that day that I care to recall. I do remember though that when

I did manage to advance the ball, as if by penalty, the ball would wind up under a leaf, never to be seen again until

the following spring. It was humbling.

The impact on my senses, though, was total, by this immensely beautiful setting. It was a golf course just out-

side Toronto, in slightly undulating terrain with a brook running through the course and mature trees lining the fair-

ways. It was a fall day, the light was beautiful as only an autumn day can produce, the air was crisp and clean and

none of the customary big city sounds such as angry horns, screeching tires and the general hum of traffic and peo-

ple was in the air. Replaced by the sound the breeze makes in the leaves and the sound of birds as they carry on

their secret conversations. I have been searching for a golf swing since that day in an attempt to justify my presence

on the golf course. After all, why should someone so inept at golf, get to use something so perfected?

Most of my golf has been played at public courses where the courses were overplayed and some of the peo-

ple running them were just putting in time. In the beginning it was for financial reasons — green fees were afford-

able — and I enjoyed meeting other people that mostly didn't play a lot better than I did. But every once in a while

I was invited to join someone for a round of golf at a country club, where golf was king. A place where the staff, from

the head pro down, knew that they worked for the members and that only the most professional attitude was acceptable. It always seemed to me that there ought to be a third category of golf venue that would combine the informality and genuineness of "regular folk" with that of a well-run golf organization that attracts respectful, genuine golf afficionados. Poppy Hills has managed to combine the best of both, and that is what first piqued my interest in this golf course, resulting in a book.

A few words about my photography. Most of the photographs taken were done under so-called ideal conditions. I waited for the shadows to be just right and spent, on some occasions, hours planning to be at a certain location just for a particular photo. In some cases only to be fogged out, or outsmarted by a golf cart. To show the different aspects to the course, I also included some photographs before sunrise, or during the many foggy periods, and I tried to catch the setting sun through the trees. Of course the dominant element of this course is the forest, which I thought would make all the holes look the same; to the designer's credit, this is not the case. There is a common theme, but each hole has its own character. Like a family.

I can only hope that as you leaf through this book, you'll be able to recall a certain shot, or an outing with one of your pals, or recount an anecdote as you look at one of the photographs. Enjoy.

Udo Machat

Village of Montclair, California

August 1998

THE AREA

*M*any people over the years have said that the Monterey Peninsula was always meant to be a golf course. This, of course, is twenty-twenty hindsight and not so much a case of destiny as it is evidence of people who made many correct decisions. Some of those were well ahead of their time, shaping and guiding the physical appearance as well as the mental outlook of everything and everyone that occupies the peninsula.

One of those people who didn't know about this destiny was Sebastian Vizcaíno. A Spanish explorer, born in 1550, he was sailing under the protection of the Count of Monte Rey, viceroy of Mexico. He was the first European to set foot on what is now the Monterey Peninsula, and named the harbor after his benefactor. The date was December 16, 1602, and on the following day, as was the custom, they went ashore, erected the church tent and said mass. This was the first mass held north of San Diego and was celebrated by Father Andrés de la Asunción.

One can only imagine the joy the fleet must have had having sailed for weeks up the coast and seeing nothing but steep cliffs. The first possible harbor would have been Carmel Bay. But as it was, for one reason or other, they passed by that bay, rounded Point Pinos and entered the second harbor. Today this is Cannery Row and the Monterey marina. The ships in the fleet were named: San Diego, San Tomás and the frigate Tres Reyes.

The voyage had been a long one, resulting in some deaths and many of the crew becoming sick with scurvy. It was decided that the San Tomás would return to Acapulco with the sick and news of the voyage as soon as repairs to the ship had been done.

Camp was set up, and the exploration of the area was started, Vizcaíno reported seeing a large number of native people, but no villages or camps. It is now believed that these native people were of the Ohlone tribe, who inhabited the coastline from Point Pinos all the way north to San Francisco. Their villages were a little inland, since the climate was more temperate. Vizcaíno described them as gentle and peaceable, generous and friendly. They came to the peninsula for gathering nuts and berries in the nearby forest and for hunting and fishing at the shore. They used nets to fish and had bow and arrows for hunting.

Explorers were in the employ of the church, and their task was to find new souls to convert for the church and new soil to till for the settlers. To this end, Vizcaíno reported to his benefactors of the countless native people, though he saw only a few with no villages, and rich soil ideal for farming, even though he stood on sand shadowed by mountains, and of a Mediterranean climate, though he was numb with cold. Might he have also been the person who invented public relations and advertising? Vizcaíno remained in the area until January 3, 1603 mapping and exploring, never to return. Not a very auspicious beginning. It should also be pointed out that Vizcaíno could not tell a mashie from a putter.

When Portolá and Crespi arrived in 1769 — one hundred and sixty-seven years later — they did

THE QUAINTNESS OF CARMEL

not recognize the surroundings from his description. Encouraged by these explorers, slowly settlers arrived in the area looking for a better life, eventually forming small settlements. Monterey, Pacific Grove and later Carmel. Walking the alley-like narrow streets of Pacific Grove, and some parts of Carmel, admiring the quaint bungalows one has to wonder why everything was done in such a constricted manner. Well, the original plots of land were measured off and sold as camp-sites, not looking far enough ahead to the possibility of permanent settlements.

By 1880 a Scottish immigrant named David Jacks had acquired title to over seven thousand acres of land. More or less the peninsula in its entirety. He donated land to the Methodist Episcopal Church, which established a Christian Seaside Resort — Pacific Grove. In the early 1880s he also sold land to the Pacific Improvement Company, which became the parent company of Del Monte Properties Company and now The Pebble Beach Company. Owned by Crocker, Hopkins, Stanford and Huntington — the "Big

Four," as they were known — had made their fortunes building railroads across the nation. Quickly a railroad line from San Francisco was laid, the Del Monte Hotel was built, and then about ten years later, the Del Monte Golf Course opened for play. The first golf course on the peninsula. World War I and the emergence of the automobile brought hard times to the Del Monte Hotel and in 1915 a man named Samuel Finley Brown Morse, in the employ of the Pacific Holding Company, was dispatched with the instructions to dissolve and liquidate the Company's interests.

The attraction of the land to the "liquidator" was immediate and rather than parcel off the property, he looked for and found financing of approximately $1.3 million, bought the property himself and formed Del Monte Properties. The year was 1919.

Possibly the most important decision he, or anyone else for that matter, made for the successful development of the peninsula was to scrap the original plan calling for home sites along Carmel Bay — what is now the seaside portion of the world famous Pebble

Beach Golf Links — and instead construct a golf course along the cliffs, with unobstructed ocean views. Temptation to immediately seek profit from the sale of home sites along the cliffs, must have been tremendous. The excitement and energy created by the roaring twenties brought great prosperity to the Del Monte venture, quickly followed by the despair of the stock market crash in 1929 and the following depression during the thirties. Before that, though, the groundwork for the inevitable success had been laid. Cypress Point Golf Course, both of the Monterey Peninsula Country Club Courses, Pacific Grove Municipal Golf Course, and Spyglass Hill Golf Course, all had the planning genius of S.F.B. Morse to thank. The land for the Poppy Hills Golf Course also was originally set aside by Del Monte Properties and Tom Fazio was retained to do a routing plan, which Robert Trent Jones Jr. followed loosely.

Instinctively, Morse had an environmental conscience that was very much ahead of the times. He had rules that positively affected all concerned — a

tree could not be planted, nor cut down, without permission — and his love for horses resulted in a system of bridle paths and the polo fields to be built. Once through the gates of the Del Monte Forest one is immediately struck with the naturalness of the whole property. This is not by accident. The events of history, as well as his personality forced the development to proceed in a restrained and orderly fashion. Samuel F.B. Morse, the "Duke of Del Monte" as he was known, passed away at the age of eighty-four on May 10, 1969.

Today Carmel, Pacific Grove and Monterey — the area even survived the closing of Fort Ord in 1995 — are thriving communities, mostly benefiting from a thriving tourist industry which for the most part is fueled by the golf courses on the peninsula. For that, a grand nephew of the man who invented the Morse code, Samuel F.B. Morse has to be thanked.

T H E   N C G A

*W*hen a game's popularity increases in as dramatic a fashion as golf has over the last few cen-turies, and especially in the last few decades, it doesn't happen without reason. In the case of golf it clearly is because of the game's versatility. It can be enjoyed by almost anyone wanting to participate. Each for their own reason. Each at their own level. One person enjoys the game for the competition, and the obvious delights in playing well. Another might enjoy the challenge of recovering from bad situations and rising to the challenge. Yet another might just enjoy simply being outdoors in usually quite beautiful, garden-like surroundings. The list is a long one and is compounded by the game's quirky nature.

One of the quirks, and reasons for the success of golf, are the "golfing societies" as they're called in the old country. On this side of the Atlantic they're called "golf associations." These early golf societies were as responsible as any other factor in the game becoming as popular as it is. Early courses were not nearly as extravagant an affair as are the country club monsters of today, where just the design fee for the architect could approach a million dollars. A typical course in those early days might have three holes and be situated on a plot of land that had lain fallow for a few years or was otherwise unsuitable for farming or grazing and hence could be used by the few individuals that had developed a craving for golf. Notice I said situated on and not built on, because these early courses were not built, unless you classify cutting a hole in the ground for the flag as building. As the game evolved, so did the expertise and the egos of the participants, requiring larger and larger plots of land in order to build larger and larger venues. This in turn made it necessary for individuals to collaborate, to pool their resources. Groups of people had an easier time getting permits and acquiring land grants. Yes, even then. In short it required a "golfing society."

The earliest evidence for golf's existence is 1413, the same year that the university was formed in St. Andrews, Scotland. The first golfing society of record is "The Honorable Company of Edinburgh Golfers" which was established a few hundred years later in 1744, and held its first annual tournament at the links of Leith that very year. It continued until 1831 when it ceased operations, but started up again in 1836 this time using the links at Musselburgh. In 1754 the St. Andrews Society of Golfers, now known as the "Royal and Ancient Golf Club" of St. Andrews, Scotland, was formed, which has given uninterrupted service to golfers worldwide as the guardian and ultimate authority on the interpretation — good or bad — of the rules of golf.

In America the development of golf courses understandably lagged behind those in Scotland and England. The first American golf club, Foxburg Country Club in Foxburg, Pennsylvania, claims activation in 1887, soon to be followed by St. Andrews Golf Club in Yonkers, New York, in 1888. It should be understood that a golf club consists of its membership and not the geographic physical location. In the case of St. Andrews Golf Club, it evolved from a three hole layout, then moved to a thirty acre site that had six holes, then moved to an apple orchard, on to a nine hole site and finally to its present location in Mt. Hope in Westchester County, New York. Quite a number of golf clubs started operations in the last two decades of the nineteenth century, most of them in the eastern part of America.

The West's first courses were Portland Golf Club in Portland, Oregon and Riverside Golf Club in Riverside, California, both of which established operations in 1894.

The United States Golf Association can trace its origins to a precise chain of events. Charles Blair Macdonald, who learned his golf in Musselburgh, Scotland, participated in the first amateur tournament sponsored by Theodore Havemeyer of the Newport Golf Club. It attracted twenty competitors and Mr. Macdonald came in second, by one stroke. When a few weeks later he was defeated on the nineteenth hole of match play at St. Andrews in Yonkers, he complained

bitterly, claiming the tournament was not executed under the rules of golf laid down by the Royal and Ancient Golf Club. His complaints were heard and listened to, resulting in the establishment of the Amateur Golf Association of the United States in 1894. It later changed its name to American Golf Association, serving both amateur and the emerging professional tour, and then to its present name: the United States Golf Association. With the USGA controlling tournaments on a national level, it created a void for local and regional associations to be organized. Some of these first associations answering the call were the Metropolitan Golf Association in 1887, the Inter-collegiate Golf Association in 1897, the Golf Association of Philadelphia in 1897, the Western Golf Association in 1899 and the SCGA, (Southern California Golf Association) in 1899.

Late in 1905, five golf clubs were instrumental in founding the Northern California Golf Association. They were: San Francisco Golf Club, Presidio Golf Course, Menlo Country Club, Claremont Country Club

THE OLD NCGA CLUBHOUSE AT SPYGLASS HILL

and Linda Vista Country Club. Shortly thereafter, Marin Golf and Country Club, Burlingame Country Club and Santa Cruz Country Club joined and might be considered founding member clubs as well. Over the next nine decades the Northern California Golf Association grew steadily, all the while serving its membership by holding, supervising and sponsoring tournaments as well as keeping the handicaps of its members. Now, the NCGA has approximately three hundred and sixty regular clubs, and seven hundred associate clubs making up the association with an individual membership of around 190,000.

What exactly was the need that was responsible for this immense success? The need was to successfully and fairly hold competitions. This meant that member courses had to be rated, allowing all individual members to compete evenly, in a variety of locations in Northern California and now across the nation. Once the courses were rated, it allowed players to be handicapped properly. In the beginning each scorecard turned in was analyzed and authenticated

by volunteers. Today players enter their score into a computer at the end of a round themselves. Printouts with computed handicaps are updated monthly and then posted in the clubhouse. In 1990 the Northern California Golf Association adopted the USGA's Slope Handicap System, in an effort to provide a nationally portable handicap system. It also follows USGA's guidelines in rating its member courses.

Proved by the success of this association one does not have to imagine how important competitions were to these original member clubs and their committees. In 1970 alone there were approximately ninety tournaments. But that didn't nearly satisfy the needs of this tournament-driven golf association, resulting in a hunger for venues that the existing courses could not satisfy. The association was staging most of its competitions at Spyglass Hill Golf Course, a course owned by Pebble Beach Company, and therefore had obligations to the resort. This resulted in scheduling conflicts. That then was the genesis for the idea of building and thereafter managing a golf course for the golf associations' purposes. With people like Bob Foley, an attorney form Albany; Charles Seaver, Francis Watson, an attorney from San Francisco; Charles Van Ling, Leslie Blue and Richard Ghent, an automobile dealer from Pebble Beach, at the helm of the association, it didn't take long before the idea of building its own facility became a plan of action. These men, all past presidents of the association, made up the board of directors in the early seventies, and decided to raise the money for the purchase of land from Pebble Beach Company by adding a surcharge to every members' handicap card. In 1977 the treasure chest had sufficiently grown to enter into a purchase agreement with Pebble Beach Company for 187 acres of land, a little up the hill from Spyglass Hill. The loan of $1.5 million was completely paid off in seven years.

John Zoller was selected to head a team to put this plan into action. John's resume is really quite spectacular — having supervised and advised on all seven courses in the Del Monte Forest — and in 1990 was honored by the American Society of Golf Course Architects as the recipient of the Donald Ross Award. This award is given to a person who has contributed to the growth, understanding and public awareness of the importance of golf course architecture to the game of golf, and was presented by Robert Trent Jones, Jr. who was president of the Society at that time.

One of the first items on the agenda was to select an architect. The short list of five architects included Robert Trent Jones, Jr., whose firm was chosen unanimously by the selection committee. Jones brought to the table a track record of being familiar with the area — his office is in nearby Palo Alto, where he worked with his father on Spyglass Hill — and an understanding of the special requirements that the location demanded. California, especially coastal California, has many environmental concerns, including the fact that the Coastal Commission would be involved in the permitting process.

Poppy Hills was the first golf course planned, constructed and now managed by an amateur golf association to be used primarily for its own functions. It was the inspiration for a few others to come, such as Massachusetts Golf Association in Boston and the Oregon Golf Association, as well as the Southern California Golf Association.

The NCGA also sponsors an internship program for golf course superintendents. Applicants chosen for the program serve a two year period at Poppy Hills or another member course. Internships are paid positions with funds budgeted from NCGA dues. In 1989 the NCGA Foundation was established in an effort to promote junior golf and also to provide assistance for turf grass research. As an example, the NCGA was the major backer to a study of the eradication of kikuyu grass.

Over the years Northern California has produced some of the world's best competitors. Men such as Tom Watson, Johnny Miller, Sandy Tatum, Harvie Ward, Ken Venturi and Stanford graduate Tiger Woods; and women such as Julie Inkster, Dr. Sally Voss of San Francisco and Sally Krueger. It is a very long list and isn't at all complete since good competition does not necessarily only mean success at the very top. Good competitions can and do happen at all levels.

When asked what makes up the soul of Poppy Hills Golf Course, John Zoller replies: "Oh, I think everything contributes to it. I think one of the unique things about it is that there are no houses on it, you know. It's pure golf, owned by an association that understands golf. It has been a tremendous success and that's because it's a pretty good course, and we do have the good fortune of being on the Monterey Peninsula. And unlike all the other courses we're not on the ocean. We have ocean views, but it's strictly an inland, forest-type golf course."

And what of the quirks of golf mentioned earlier? Well, my brother, who is a non-golfing European, has a big problem grasping the concept of equating the minus sign with excellence.

Well, I've tried to explain, but...

THE DESIGNERS

*T*he very first golf courses were not designed; they had a beginning — a driving area, and they had a finish — a hole in the ground. No par, no artificially placed and constructed obstacles, no island greens and no real estate developments to finance the development. In fact, it was probably a pasture that one of the players happened to own, and the grass in the fairway was only shorter because the sheep preferred it. It wasn't until the 1880s that someone actually was paid to design and construct a golf course. Today, some of the more prominent architects, whose names will help in the promotional and sales activities of the development, ask for and receive enormous fees.

During this evolutionary time however there were men who defined the profession for little pay. Men who had families, and had to earn a living to support them. Since paying for design services was not a common occurrence, these early designers had to be flexible and creative in their ways of educating potential clients about their expertise, and justifying a fee for it.

Such a man was Robert Trent Jones. He started caddying at the Rochester Country Club, New York, at fourteen. Not for the love of the game but for the need of hard cash. The love came soon enough when he started to play and play well. He entered the occasional amateur tournament and was named the most promising young golfer in the Rochester area at age sixteen. Sadly, he developed an ulcer, putting his competitive golf on hold for a few years. During that time Trent Jones decided that competitive golf was not for him, and took a job at a golf course in Sodus Bay, New York, as the golf pro. His job description however also included that of greenkeeper and manager of the club. He was a busy young man.

During this time he watched Donald Ross build Oak Hill in Rochester, and thought that this was something he would like to do, since he couldn't play competitive golf. With the help of James Bashford, who was a member at Sodus Country Club, he entered Cornell University, creating a program for himself, a curriculum comprising of the subjects a golf course designer would have to be fluent in: hydraulics, surveying, agronomy, horticulture, economics, chemistry, public speaking, journalism, business law and sketching. During his second year at Cornell he met Ione Tefft Davis, who would become his wife and life partner. He finished his studies at Cornell University in 1930, aged 24.

He managed to get a few remodeling jobs, and then his first major assignment, for which he was not paid since the club went bankrupt before the work was finished. It was to design a course for the Midvale Golf and Country Club near Rochester, New York. Midvale also called in a very competent Canadian architect named Stanley Thompson to share in the design work. Eventually Thompson and Jones formed a partnership that lasted until 1938. They worked on many courses in Canada and in South America. It was post-depression and the times were hard, requiring an inventive mind to promote projects since money was a scarce commodity. Those that had it did not want to part with it. This then was the world that Robert Trent Jones, Jr. was born into in 1939.

Those years and the next several until 1945 were rough with all that was going on in the world at the time. But then "Bobby Jones," the famous amateur golfer from Georgia, chose Robert Trent Jones to design Peachtree Golf Club in Atlanta. This changed his life forever. Giving him his biggest assignment to date and with his involvement with the other Jones, a name change. Robert Trent Jones thought there should only be one Bob Jones and hence chose to be called Trent Jones. Jones' career was off and running and now in his nineties is closing in on 500 courses designed or remodeled. He has built or remodeled many of the courses on which the US Open and the PGA have been contested. Courses such as: Oakland Hills, Baltusrol, Firestone, Bellerive, Oak Hill, Olympic Club and Hazeltine.

Bobby, Jr., as the son came to be called, had by all accounts a quite normal childhood. The family home was in Montclair, New Jersey, where Bobby at age seven had the weekly grass cutting chores. One day his dad came home and gruffly told his son that he had lost out on a possible assignment because the lawn, which his prospective client had seen, had not been groomed well enough. This may have been Bobby's first brush with the golf course design business. He attended Yale, and graduated in 1961. He was a member of Yales' Eastern Intercollegiate Championship Golf Team. On to Stanford Law School, for a year. Just long enough to find out that the law was not for him, so he joined his dad's firm in 1962. His younger brother Rees also joined the firm two years after that. During the next dozen years, the firm was very busy. Bobby co-designed quite a few courses with his dad. They had opened a west coast office, in Palo Alto, and Bobby worked on Spyglass Hill Golf Course on the Monterey Peninsula. Bobby had always had an environmental conscience, and with newly emerging environmental concerns, the California Coastal Commission, and especially the fragile nature

FOG STARTS TO CREEP THROUGH THE TREES AT THE OPENING HOLE

of the Monterey Peninsula, this conscience became a very central requirement for successfully working in this part of the world.

For various reasons Bobby, and Rees left the design office of Trent Jones around 1974 to set up their own firms. In hindsight its easy to see that this was necessary in order for each to build on their own individual reputations. Bobby has now been credited with the design and construction of more than one hundred and fifty new and remodeled golf courses around the world. He has been an active member of the American Society of Golf Course Architects since 1966, and served as the Society's president in 1989–90. In 1982–83 he was chairman of the California State Park and Recreation Commission. In 1991 he was inducted into the California Golf Hall of Fame. In 1987, USA Today selected sixteen of Mr. Jones' courses for inclusion in its list of the best courses in the United States built after 1962. Quite an accomplished career.

And what of design philosophies? Trent Jones says of his son Bobby: "Bobby is the quintessential naturalist, letting the land dictate the design of his holes and courses. His creations are sometimes more flamboyant than mine, but he always does a wonderful job of blending his work with the surroundings. His holes and courses are in harmony with the environment. He considers golf an outdoor chess game and so puts great emphasis on the mental aspects of the game. His courses tend to be more strategic, with some mixture of penal and heroic holes. Bobby believes that all elements of the game — strength, accuracy, club selection and finesse — should be tested; that a Ben Crenshaw should not be allowed to win just because he's the best putter."

It goes without saying that a designer could design a layout that would be impossible to play. Length and obstacles could be placed in such a way that even the most skilled player would have no chance of being successful. That's not the goal though. What is in the designer's mind is to skillfully, sometimes even imperceptibly, introduce elements that will test the players' expertise, and expand their abilities.

You won't know whether you can successfully carry a ball for two hundred yards over a brush-infested barranca late in the day until you're forced to.

The relationship of golf course architect and the players and competitors who use their creations might be that of a benevolent dictator to his admiring subjects. Mussolini's name comes to mind. The architect judges the abilities of the players and the capabilities of their equipment, listens to the needs of the people commissioning his services, and studies the land that Mother Nature provides. Duly considers all this, and comes up with a product that will delight players on a good, and confound them on a bad day. All the while stretching the envelope a little. A phrase linked with Bobby's dad is, "a hole should be designed so that it will yield a hard par and an easy bogey."

The architects, lonely and misunderstood as they are, do have a need for the golfing public to appreciate their efforts though. For the designer it's not enough anymore to offer these strategic choices, extend an invitation for a mental battle, unless the players actually comprehend and appreciate the choices and design nuances offered. This has little to do with how well a player has mastered the physical part of the game — there are any number of books available on that subject — but it has everything to do with how well the competitors understand the design of the architect. To this end Bobby has written a book titled *"Golf by Design,"* in which he talks about golf course design features available to the architect, offering the reader insights into the creator's mind. It would be Bobby's contention that in order to play the course well, one really does have to understand the options available before starting the round.

At Poppy Hills Jones used four basic design elements for the layout of the course. Large greens, unique bunkers, split fairways and multiple tees. The multiple tees can vary the length of a hole by as much as fifty yards, from the back tees. Shorter hitting players were not overlooked, changing the length of their tee positions by as much as a hundred yards in some cases. The greens are much larger than the proportion of the holes would dictate. This was one of the main features that John Zoller and his committee required, in order to accommodate a large number of players and still be able to offer each a fair putting surface. The greens do suffer with heavy play. Jones says about the large greens: "We start with the idea that large greens are more practical and useful when the course is subjected to heavy traffic. But more to the point, people think that the target in golf is the green. It's not. The hole is the target. So building large greens is not necessarily an evil. If one can accept that, then one can break the green into two or three different areas, quite separate from one another, which is the key to providing a variety of golfing options." This can result in some very long putts, putts that may have to navigate across picturesque undulations and sometimes extreme inclines. In the original design these elevation changes in some instances were much more severe than they are today. After the initial five year trial period, the association came to the conclusion that some of the greens were too penal, and conse-

quently eased some of the tougher ones. To help the golfer out a little, most greens are constructed like saucers, higher at the edges to gather shots. The fairways are divided into individual smaller targets by center bunkering, and by crossing rough. This creates a stage for an aerial game, a positional game that has to be accurate, with not any one approach necessarily being the correct one. A player can mostly play a hole from his strength and overcome a possible weakness. Can we all identify with this?

Bobby Jones' name is on the course as the architect, but naturally, a great number of people are involved to produce this firms' world-class layouts. Most notably is the chief designer, Don Knott. Don came to join Bobby in Palo Alto in 1973 and has been the lead designer on numerous courses, including Poppy Hills. Around the world he has been involved in approximately fifty golf courses to date. Don is an active member of the American Society of Golf Course Architects, and served as the Society's president for one term starting in 1994. He received a bachelor's degree in Landscape Architecture from the University of California at Berkeley in 1969, and a Masters degree in Architecture form the same University in 1973. If that weren't enough, this local boy who was born in Alameda, managed to make the varsity swim team, became an All-American in 1966 and served two years in the U.S. Army. With credentials such as these I have no problem putting the words, excellence, Don Knott and Poppy Hills all in one sentence.

The responsibilities of the lead designer are many. First, and perhaps most important, is the routing which is a close collaboration between Bobby and his senior designer. Naturally, the final layout only shows the option chosen, with many others explored, critiqued and rejected for one reason or another. Early on this happens casually, between Don and Bobby and other associates and later more earnestly and finally with the client in attendance. All the while producing drawings, drawings and more drawings. Plans for irrigation and drainage are just two of the many invisible necessities of a golf courses infrastructure that are considered. On to the construction phase which for the lead designer is a hands-on, on-site proposition, cutting trees to lay bare fairways, guiding bulldozers to shape the land and finesse and massage the greens, the sowing of grass and the planting of flowers.

That's where a well coordinated experienced construction and landscape crew become essential. Robert Trent Jones II is one of just a few architects who operates his own construction company. Called Greenscape, this company oversees or builds Bobby's courses. Bud Sexten was the president of Greenscape during the construction of Poppy Hills. Bud says: "Building golf courses has been my life's work, first for Mr. Jones, Sr. and now for Bobby."

This dedication to the job seems to run rampant among all who are active in the golf industry. I have an idea that everyone feels extremely privileged in having some small part in it, and making "the game" even better.

SAND — SOMETIMES ORNAMENTAL, SOMETIMES PENAL, ALWAYS TROUBLE

THE COURSE

*A*t a time when the construction of golf courses was in its infancy and the profession of golf

course architect was nearly unheard of, a man named George Crump accepted the task of

designing and supervising the construction of a golf course near Philadelphia. This was a time

when the equipment available to golfers was in its infancy also. Golf clubs had wooden shafts,

were combined into a set not by numbers but by their personality, and golf balls did not go very

far by today's standards. His task was to design the ultimate golf challenge. Here is what he

thought this golf course should aspire to: "First, four one-shot holes, these to be well separated

and two on each nine, to suit the four principal clubs — a mashie, a mid-iron, a cleek or spoon,

and a full all-out driver. Then a genuine drive and pitch hole and a drive and pitch and run hole.

Two holes, one on each nine, well separated, with exceptionally long second shots to get home.

Also two three-shot holes, nicely separated, and never to be reached in two shots. Also, four holes of the drive and mid-iron variety, well-placed, two with bunkers in front and two with some open way to the green. And four more designed in length for good healthy second shots after a good but not necessarily unusual drive — the greens open on two but with bunkers in front of, or threatening, on the two others." These were George Crump's personal requirements for a tough test of golf and became the blueprint used to create the Pine Valley Golf Club.

At Poppy Hills no one wants to take credit for being "George Crump," even though someone obviously was the first to have the spark of an idea to build the course. But certainly once a few of the NCGA members started talking about it, the wish list was well on its way. And what might that list have been? To be sure, if success was to be attained the course had to fit the needs of the association. That need was not to build the toughest challenge, but to challenge the ability to play the game, of all who stepped up to the first tee. This required that all holes had to have a number of separate tee locations, since length off the tee is one

of the first differences between levels of expertise. Especially when forced carries were involved, all players had to be considered, and once on the green there had to be flagstick placements that would be easily negotiated and others that would be a challenge to the best. The course would serve as the venue for many amateur tournaments, and since 1988 has served as one of the four courses used in the AT&T Pebble Beach National Pro-Am, which brings the best of the best to the Monterey Peninsula each year in February.

John Zoller, one of those involved from the beginning, when asked about the course's flexibility, says: "Well, you know, I think the course is very flexible. For instance, I'm also a member at Monterey Peninsula Country Club, and we have two courses over there, and my wife plays both of them and Poppy Hills a lot. On the face of it, you would think that for women the Country Club's two courses would be much easier, but they're not. They're much more difficult for women, because at that time women were not considered at the design stage, therefore the course design did not address their needs. Such as forced carries and things like that. As a consequence all current designs for golf courses have great flexibility in the tee locations, multiple tees and the landing areas making it conducive to women players, high-handicap players, seniors as well as accomplished players. It can be fun for the amateurs and a challenge to the professional."

Poppy Hills has the unique distinction of being the only course on the Monterey Peninsula that is situated entirely in the forest. All others touch the ocean in one way or another. As I strolled around the course the other day, I believe I only caught sight of the ocean twice. And even then, it might have been the top of a fog bank rather than the water itself that I saw. The fog does roll in, not as it does at the shore, where the wind pushes it unobstructed as a white unmanaged mass. Here it seems to catch itself in the trees, first appearing a little at a time as if to spy, then more and more. The fog also changes sound; all of a sudden the birds' talk is no longer melodious but haunting, and the mut-

terings of your playing partner are not nearly as distinct. But when the sun is out, the course is quite different. The fragrance of freshly cut grass intermingles with that of the trees and is not at all of the same vintage as the kelp and sea odors a few hundred feet below at the shore of Monterey Bay.

Most golf courses have two par threes, two par fives and five par fours on the front and then the very same combination on the back nine. Poppy Hills Golf Course is a par 72, with five par fives and five par threes and only eight par fours. There are two consecutive par fives interrupted only by a stop at the snack bar after number nine. After the tenth, a par three, and on to a par five again. Jones says: "The reason for this is the way the land was shaped. It worked out better that way on the land we found. I was more interested in the holes working well than in being rigidly orthodox."

The tone for development respecting the environment on the Monterey Peninsula was set very early by Samuel F.B. Morse. Under his leadership, he was

DISTRACTIONS WHOSE BEAUTY LIVE IN THE DETAILS

well ahead of the times, development was only allowed to go forward at a very slow pace. Always in mind was the fragile surrounding and how new elements introduced would affect the whole. These same concerns were also adopted by the planners of Poppy Hills. Along the twelfth fairway is a stand of Gowan Cypress that are only found in this area and are protected by environmental concerns. In fact, that area to the right of the twelfth fairway was declared out of bounds to ensure that golfers would not unwittingly trample on and hurt this species of tree. Soil with poor nutrients is the cause for the stunted growth of these Gowan Cypress and to ensure that nutrients from the fairway did not alter the natural development of these trees, runoff from the fairway was diverted.

A project the size of a golf course has some very permanent effects on the land it occupies and the surrounding communities. There is a long list of governmental agencies involved to get all the permissions necessary before construction can begin. When a golf course is in California and close to the ocean, the all powerful Coastal Commission must be involved. Not surprisingly, it took almost five years for this permitting process to be completed. It was quite fortuitous that a man named Myron E. Etienne, Jr., an attorney from Salinas, was found. He was as central to the success of this project as anyone, since he made obstacles presented by committees disappear in mid-air. John Zoller says: "I think without Myron we would never have been successful in getting all our permits. He was able to procure a Negative Declaration, making it unnecessary to do an Environmental Impact Report. Unheard of, but we got one."

One of the immediate benefits of carving a course from the forest as Poppy Hills, is that one is left with mature trees bordering the fairways. On opening day, the impression was of a course that had been played for years and years. The only down side to this might be that golfers are robbed of becoming acquainted with critical obstacle-forming trees at an early age. Few would object, but think of all the tall tales that never saw the light of day. A good example of this is on the tenth hole, where a tree guards the green from an heroic second shot to the green. And again, the same situation on the finishing hole. In both cases, though, the trees were left untouched by the designers in order to steer the player to safer ground, according to Don Knott. Don goes on to say that trees in general, no matter how strong and solid they are, should not be used as the sole design element, since they are not permanent.

A benefit to playing a hole that is completely surrounded by trees is that the job to be done is spelled out rather clearly. The holes seem to welcome and embrace all who visit. The sound, too, is trapped within the confines of the fairways, making a crisp shot reverberate off the trees for all to hear. When a golf ball is hit well, a player knows immediately by how the club felt in his hands at impact. A badly hit ball will almost always fight back and hurt. In a much more subtle way, sound also tells of the difference between a well-hit or a badly-hit shot. Hopefully we have all delighted to the sound of a crisply hit golf ball.

Early in the design evolvement of golf clubs, specialty clubs such as the sand wedge did not exist. At that time having to play your ball from sand was a definite penalty. With the invention of "bounce," which helps the club skim through the sand, tournament and most club players do not look on it as a hazard any more, but actually prefer it to being in the deep grass that often surrounds a green. At Pine Valley, whose membership take pride in the fact that it is the acknowledged toughest and most uncompromising golf course on the face of the earth, a player attempted to putt out of a sand trap and failed. Not an uncommon approach when the conditions are right. What was unusual though is that he was told, had he succeeded, the face of the trap would have been promptly steepened to prevent this from happening again. At Poppy Hills Golf Course the approach to this is slightly more benign.

At Poppy Hills the greens are mostly quite large, and in the original design were split into "compartments" by raising and lowering portions to form separate entities making it possible for the green keepers to place the flagstick in many different locations, allowing the greens to recover nicely from the heavy play this busy course gets. This, however, was interpreted as making the greens too tough since when a player had hit a poor shot to the green and was nowhere near the flagstick he now had to negotiate a putt that had two opposite breaks, a twenty foot long uphill, blending into a ten foot long downhill... well, you get the idea.

The designers of this course had decided early on that the game should not end with an easy two-putt, having reached the green in regulation. Rather, the green would present its own challenges in reading the various factors, assembling them in your mind and then calling on your body to execute as planned. In a book published in 1887, when the technology of golf course design and construction had not been elevated to the lofty plateau of the 1990s, a Sir W.G. Simpson wrote a book titled *"The Art of Golf,"* in which he writes: "It is in putting, more than in any other part of the game, that the would-be medal winners, and those who enter to see what they will do, are apt to fail on medal days. Bad driving, with a turn of luck, may lose you little or nothing; but bad putting runs up a score that you will only reveal to inquiring friends after one or two askings and some explanation as to what bad luck you had." It is interesting that even at that time luck was an acknowledged ingredient to the game. More specifically, bad luck, when one's talents did not measure up to what needed to be done.

The agreement between Jones and the Northern California Golf Association was to let the course remain as designed for five years and then evaluate possible changes. Which is exactly what happened. John Zoller says: "The changes were pretty much handled in-house. Some of the greens — and I don't want this to sound like criticism of Jones' design — but all the architects at that time, Jones, Palmer etc., all of them were creating greens that were much more undulating. They have all returned to much more subtle designs in the last few years. But at that time they were all doing very dramatic elevation changes and we just felt that in the interest of play and to produce a better playing surface, we would modify some of the contours. Along with that we also modified some of the bunkering, which we felt was more severe than needed to test the skills of a player."

The daily upkeep of a course is one of the more challenging aspects to running a golf course. Just think of the quirky nature of the weather — especially in the last few years. When the usual problem is not enough water, and where to get it, it has been a situation of how to drain the course of it. Manny Sousa is the man who has been at the helm as course superindendant for most of the years, since the course opened in 1985. The greens are poa annua, and the association likes them fast. 9.5 on the stimp meter. The rough is planted in rye, and the fairways in colonial bent. It is the aim of Manny Sousa and his staff of sixteen, to keep the course in near tournament condition year round. For the yearly AT&T the preparations start two to three months ahead of the tournament.

Not so much to prepare the playing surfaces, but more in special preparations to accommodate the gallery.

The course also features a more than adequate driving range, a very nice putting green and tucked in behind the entry gate to the right a chance to practice escapes from the sand. Few players see it necessary to walk to this slightly out of the way practice area though. The pro shop is kept stocked with anything a player might want or need and the restaurant serves good, inexpensive fare. A very nice place to relive the round with your group.

Paul Porter is the president and CEO of Poppy Hills Golf Course. Bob Higgins is a member of the PGA and is director of golf and Tyler Jones is the PGA head professional. This is the management that makes your experience at the golf course as enjoyable as possible. Call 408-625-2035 to book tee times. I'm sure they would love to hear from you.

TREES, MORE TREES AND BRUSH

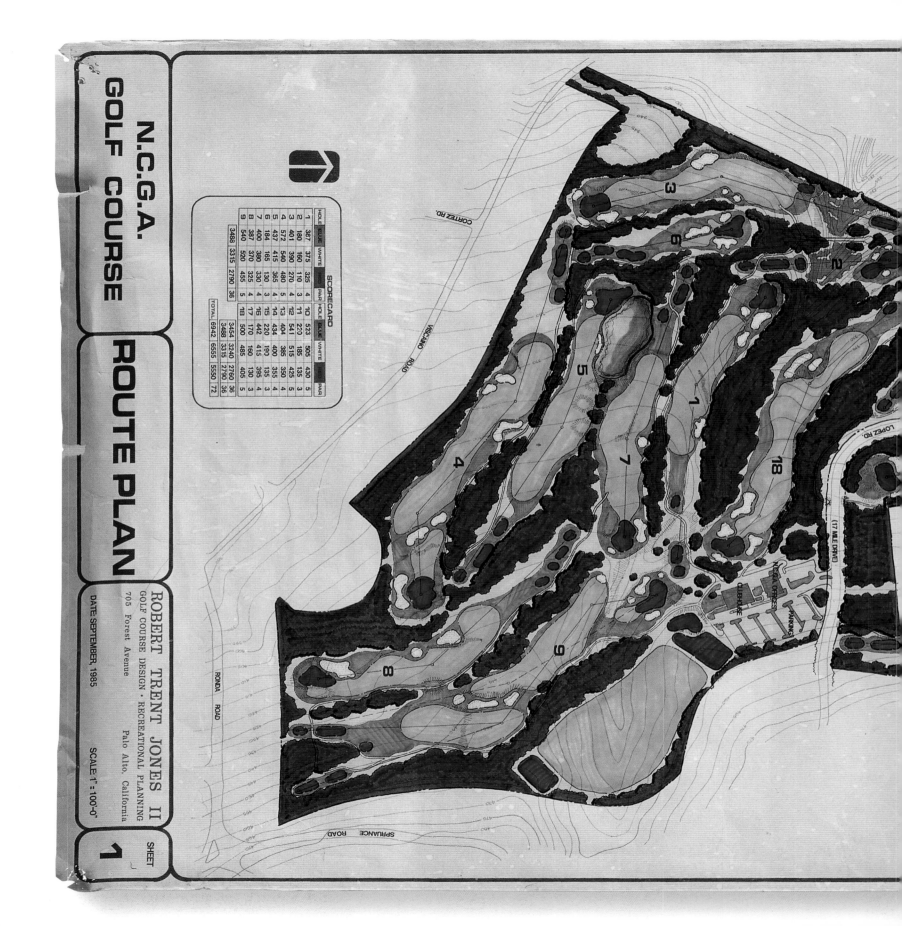

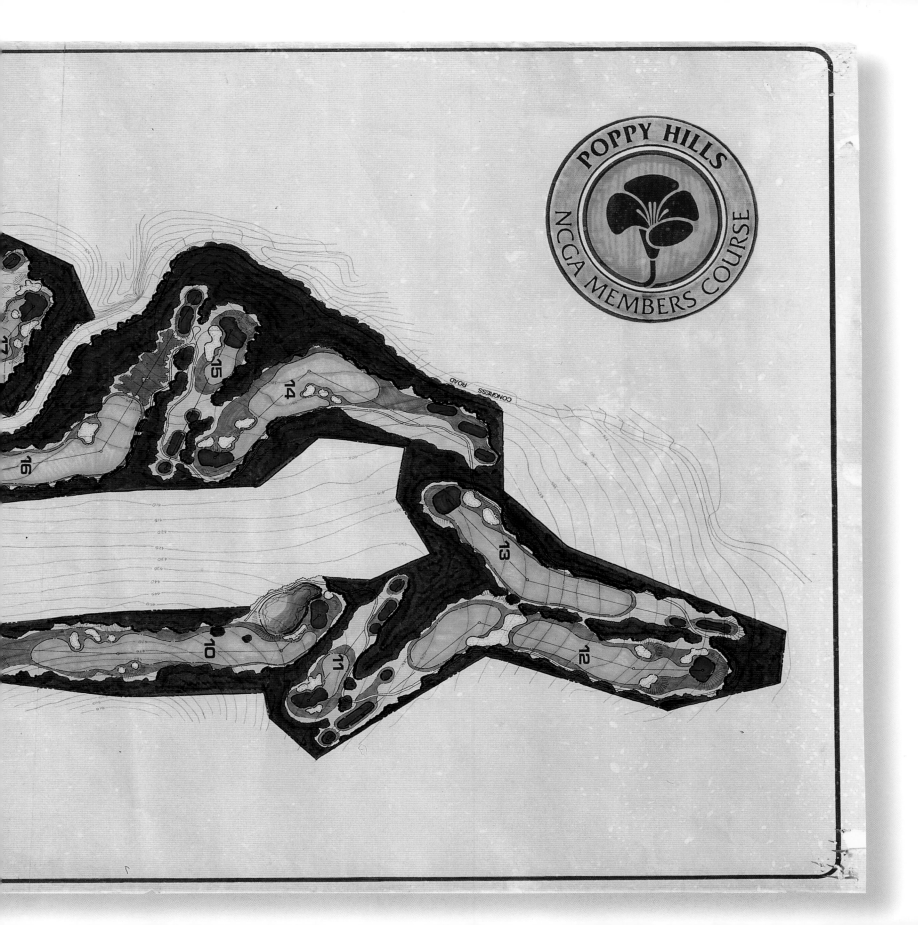

No.1 413 YARDS PAR 4

*A*t first examination, this hole seems to have a shape that is exactly as the average golfer would like to find on an opening hole. A hole that's slightly downhill and apparently able to accept a slice without too much difficulty. But, it is one of the more difficult holes of the course, because of its length and more importantly because of the steep ravine to the right. A ball that enters this maze of brush and wooden limbs is probably lost, or unplayable. The short bunker on the right was placed there in an attempt to force the player away from doom and into the fairway. Long hitters have a chance to attack the hole from the left side of the fairway, by catching the downslope and adding even more yards to the drive. The landing area, unfortunately, also has a lot of undulations to further complicate this first hole. The second shot to the green will have to carry all the way to the green, since a series of bunkers in front make bouncing the ball to the flag virtually impossible. Once on the green, you will find some very severe undulations. As we said before, this hole is an eye-opener. You've got to have your game ready when you step up to the tee at this hole.

HELPFUL HINT: Don't be shy; it's only a game.

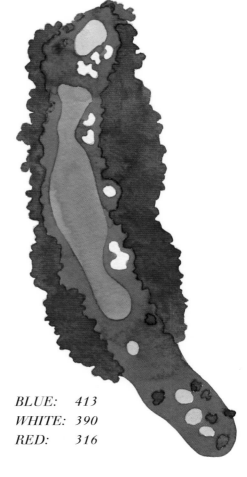

BLUE: 413
WHITE: 390
RED: 316

No. 2   174 YARDS   PAR 3

*T*he same ravine you've become familiar with on the first hole, hopefully from a respectable distance, is now right in front of you cutting across your shot to the green. From the back tees you can't see it; but then if you're at the back tees this shouldn't intimidate you. From the front you're looking right down this ravine. It can't possibly be a good

thing. This also is a forced carry, since anything short by a foot or two will roll back and down. The green was originally designed as one large green with two levels. Today, the grass is mowed to create two separate areas, separated by a terrace that runs across it diagonally. Obviously the front is the easier, because of the lesser distance, with the back green becoming even more challenging than just the additional yardage, but because of the added threat of deep bunkers and the very steep bank on the left. This hole has a lot of flexibility, since it can play 110 yards one day and 174 yards the next.

HELPFUL HINT: Be calm and hit the shot you're capable of.

BLUE: *174*
WHITE: *142*
RED: *110*

No. 3   406 YARDS   PAR 4

*T*his hole requires that your arsenal of shots include a draw. From the tee the green is hidden behind the trees on the left. Visible is the same ravine that has dictated shots on the first two holes. It doesn't really come into play other than as a psychological obstacle. With anything other than a draw, the ball will, upon landing, bounce toward the right side. With a fade the ball will disappear forever right in front of your eyes. The ideal shot is a slight draw, that stays very close to the trees on the left. When the course was first opened, there were a series of pot bunkers at that point, giving the better players a point to carry. The photograph on page 66 shows one of those pot bunker in the foreground. But those bunkers proved to be too intimidating for the average golfer, hence they were pulled out. The second shot is slightly uphill to a green that has several levels and is well bunkered on the left and the back. This green has an opening at the front, allowing the player to bounce the ball onto the putting surface.

HELPFUL HINT: Don't forget my friend, the greens are large. Take aim on the flagstick.

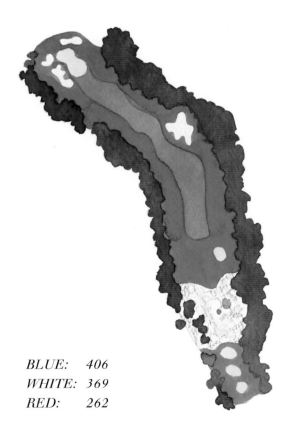

BLUE: *406*
WHITE: *369*
RED: *262*

No.4   560 YARDS   PAR 5

*T*his hole is the longest par five at Poppy Hills but is reachable in two — for those that hit the ball long and straight. The trap on the right is the aim since you have to carry it to have a chance at a long second shot to the green. Additionally you have to be toward the right side for a semi-unobstructed second shot, which will probably have to be a draw. It does take two good, as well as differently shaped, shots to be on the green for that elusive eagle. For those of us who only dream of such feats, the trap on the left is the aim, with a slight fade. The second shot then once again to the trap on the left with a little draw or right over it to a small landing area. The green is very large and undulating, therefore a short third shot is a definite bonus. The shape of the green allows flagstick positions that are tucked into little protuberances. Once again, the flag is the target, not the green. From front to back the green is approximately forty steps. Around the green, there are bunkers to the right that make uninvited guests reflect on the virtues of practicing shots out of sand. Some could be at rather long distances.

HELPFUL HINT: Putting is something we can all improve.

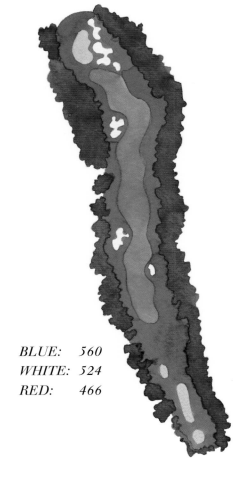

BLUE: 560
WHITE: 524
RED: 466

No. 5 426 YARDS PAR 4

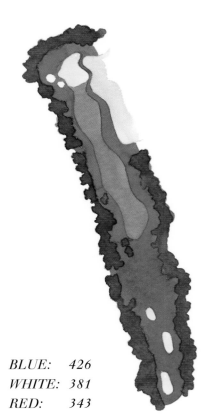

A straight hole with water. Poppy Hills has water on only three of the eighteen holes. It is, after all, in the forest on the top of a hill. From the golfer's perspective this hole is slightly downhill with a gentle left to right slope. A lengthy tee shot could actually find the water on the right. But from the tee it seems to be straight ahead. Ideally, a slight draw winding up close to the trees on the left will give you the position required for a second shot to a green that can have some very tough flagsticks. There are a few mounds on the right side of the fairway that were put in to penalize a push. The green has two pot bunkers guarding the short left side, with a ridge running obliquely across the green. It has a left to right slope which will allow you to run a ball all the way to the back. The upper level is the preferred area for flagstick positions with the toughest in the back — a peninsula. When the flagstick is there, water is on your mind when you stand over your ball. *Bonne chance, monsieur.* Go over the green and you'll be playing on a very steep bank.

HELPFUL HINT: Be advised, the water is reachable from the tee.

BLUE: 426
WHITE: 381
RED: 343

No.6   181 YARDS   PAR 3

*T*his medium length par three is slightly downhill. You would normally be hitting into the prevailing wind coming off the ocean. This is also the only hole where a glimpse of the ocean appears behind the green. The green is framed by the ever present Monterey Pine; should you be lucky enough to be there late in the day with the sunlight filtering through the trees you'll have good memories — no matter what the score. More often than not though, this spectacular sunlight is replaced with fog. This too, is spectacular in its own manner. As always with a crisp, confident swing that sends the ball to its rightful place — the green — there shouldn't be too much trouble here. However just in case, there are traps to the left and right and a third in front of the green. The ball has to be carried to this green which has several plateaus to accommodate various flagstick positions. The putting surface is surrounded by grass that is fairway cut, so that your ball will roll down the slope leaving you with a sometime awkward chip back to the flagstick. A shot that is short in the front may run down thirty feet for instance.

HELPFUL HINT: Don't pay attention to the scenery — yet.

BLUE: 181
WHITE: 141
RED: 120

No.7   388 YARDS   PAR 4

One of the shorter par fours is a gentle dogleg left that plays uphill. From the tee, searching for the green, your eyes will focus on a pot bunker that is in a straight line to the flagstick. That bunker is placed there for exactly that purpose. To serve as a target. It helps analyze the problem at hand and that is probably the first step towards a confident decision on how to play this medium length par four. The reservoir that was very dominant on the fifth hole is to the right, but should not come into play. The fairway has a slight left to right slope, therefore the ideal position is the left side, close to the pot bunker. A ball hit to the right will of course bounce further to the right. Should you, however, wind up on this side, then a grassy hollow by the side of the green comes into play. Your second shot will have to be very accurate to get near the flagstick. Behind the green we have a dramatic drop into the swale we've seen on numbers one, two, three and will see again at nine and eighteen. Should your ball have gone there, you'll have a shot to the flag, even though it might be twenty feet above your head.

HELPFUL HINT: Are you having fun yet?

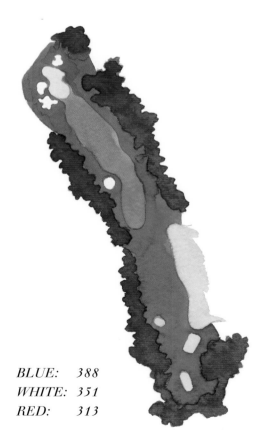

BLUE: 388
WHITE: 351
RED: 313

No. 8   390 YARDS   PAR 4

*O*ne of the first holes to be built, it is also one of the prettier ones. It is an extreme dogleg right, with a bunker at the turn that is surrounded by tall Monterey Pine. Clearly not the place to be. But as if it were a magnet, it attracts many customers. You might consider using an iron as your weapon *du jour,* since your driver could send your ball through the fairway on the left and into the trees. From the tee, the green cannot be seen, but there doesn't seem to be a question as to where it is. As you walk along the fairway to your ball, soon the green appears. And what a beautiful setting for the putting surface. From the turning point it's downhill by about thirty feet. The green is two-tiered with the edge of the upper plateau running more or less perpendicular to your second shot. To the right and short is a large flower-shaped sand formation that one should stay clear of. Behind the green, the terrain falls off very quickly and the left side rolls off into a tightly mowed fairway area making it essential to play a shot that holds the green.

HELPFUL HINT: Start thinking about longer destinations.

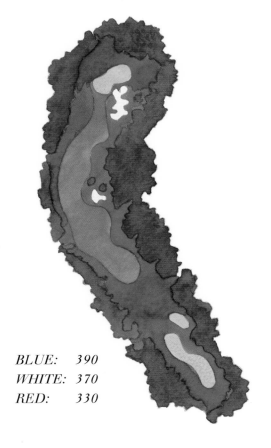

BLUE: 390
WHITE: 370
RED: 330

No. 9   557 YARDS   PAR 5

*T*his hole exemplifies the thought behind the Poppy Hills Golf Course design. It gives the player options. It allows the player to plan the attack. The hole can be played aggressively or safely, and is designed with two teeing areas. The first one, reached on your way from the eighth green, is slightly shorter and makes the layout a double dogleg.

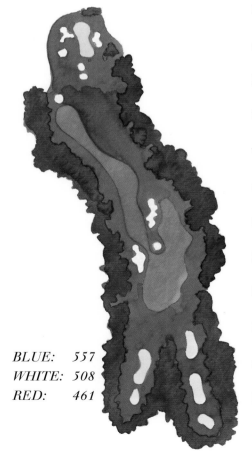

Further up the hill to the second tee and you'll have a slightly longer but straighter hole. If the fairway weren't uphill you could probably spy the flag in line with a pot bunker right in the middle of the fairway. At that pot bunker, the fairway splits into two levels. The long hitters going for the green in two will have to carry that bunker plus the next one. For the more moderate players, being in one of the bunkers is not the kiss of death, but a chance to show that advancing the ball from a sandy lie is part of your game. From here the fairway actually turns away from the green, following the contour of the swale that runs across the hole. The green is two-tiered, not too wide but quite long. Ideal to accept a screaming three wood. Two pot bunkers to the front and one on each side keep you honest.

HELPFUL HINT: Plan your shots well in advance. It will pay off.

BLUE: 557
WHITE: 508
RED: 461

No. 10   511 YARDS   PAR 5

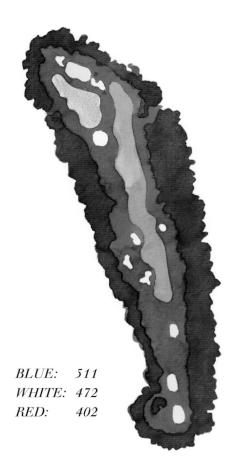

*A*nother short par five. As on the previous hole, the long hitting player, with good execution, can reach the green in two. But there are some obstacles to that plan. First, the tee shot is blind, uphill to a fairly steep side slope even though a lot of earth was moved from what is now the right edge of the fairway. The bunkers on the left will encourage players to send their balls to the right in order to catch a fairly narrow landing strip. The forest as usual is quite unforgiving. In fact, the undergrowth here is thick. Your second shot needs to be quite accurate as well, in both, direction and length. This is the only other time that water comes into play at Poppy Hills. You have two options: stay short of the water, avoiding interference from a large Monterey Pine, or go a little further to the right of the water to a very skimpy landing area. The second choice will line you up for a very easy shot to the green; the first will make the shot to the green over water to a narrow target. The green is situated in a bowl, hence a shot a little right or long has a good chance of curling onto the green. The green has two levels and allows for many interesting flagsticks.

HELPFUL HINT: Watch out for the water, *mon capitaine.*

BLUE: 511
WHITE: 472
RED: 402

No.11　214 YARDS　PAR 3

*T*his is the longest of the five par threes, if only by a few yards. From the tee the golfer sees a sliver of differently colored grass — that's the green. It takes up a lot of room from left to right. It seems to be big. It isn't. The green is placed obliquely to the shot, with very little depth. It has three levels and many more flagstick positions. All of them require accurate shots if you want to putt for a birdie. There are two traps on the right and one on the left. The left side of the green falls off steeply, that should the green be missed, the ball will roll down and away from the green. It could be a difficult pitch back to the flagstick, since the grass can be deep on occasion. A ball hit low and short can actually run onto the green, but probably not to a back flagstick. There can easily be a two-club difference between the front and back tiers. The back tier naturally is the toughest flagstick position, posing the problem of having to carry the entire bunker on the right as well as being accurately on line to avoid missing the green altogether. Once on the green and on the proper level, you'll find yourself putting without too much doubt. The green is very true.

HELPFUL HINT: Take one more club, and do swing easy.

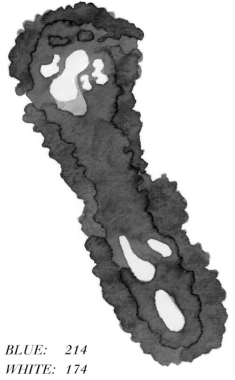

BLUE:　*214*
WHITE:　*174*
RED:　　*151*

No.12 531 YARDS PAR 5

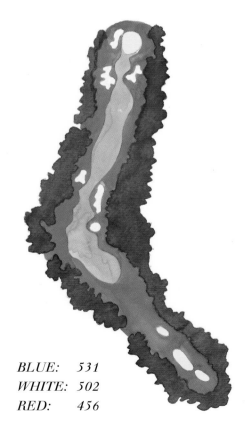

BLUE: 531
WHITE: 502
RED: 456

*W*ith a superb tee shot, this is another par five that's reachable in two. Emphasis on superb. It is an extreme dog-leg to the right requiring a high cut shot over the pot bunker and beside the trap on the side of the fairway to set up a second shot to the green. It's a dangerous shot since the whole right side is out of bounds — to protect a dwarf cypress grove — but should it work, you'll feel good until tomorrow. When the course was first opened, this area was a cross bunker that defied anyone to carry. Well, maybe now there is such a man. The next shot to the green is tough too; you're looking at a narrow gap flanked by two traps with the green beyond. For the normal person, the first shot to the corner, next shot short of the bunkers and a nine iron to the flagstick. That also has a good ring, doesn't it? The green has several levels. The back level is flat, making it difficult to hold a shot that's hit to the flagstick. The back and right sides are fairly steep and are usually covered by deep grass. This hole is a definite example of how the designer offers you choices and makes you decide on a plan of action. But, the decision has to be made at the tee.

HELPFUL HINT: Pause half-way and look at the dwarf cypress.

No.13 393 YARDS PAR 4

*F*rom the tee you'll see a simple-looking hole. A slight curve to the right, no bunkers to worry about and a fairly wide fairway. Let 'er rip. Of course, make sure you stay in the fairway because no matter how benign, the rough — well, it makes it rough. The hole just follows the natural terrain, and with the trees mature, it seems that the hole has always been just the way you see it now. For most players the hole plays long enough, especially when you consider that it is a little uphill. To the front and right of the green are two three-pronged sand bunkers. From the fairway it is possible to be confused and forget that the bunker you see is actually thirty yards in front of the green. Now that I look at the second bunker, it does seem to have a smirk in its design. Many golfers have made that mistake and paid. The bunkers have steep sides and the green can be quite distant. Once on the green, you'll see two distinct levels and three mounds that define the putting surface. There can be some very tough flagstick positions. Not only to hit to, but to putt to as well.

HELPFUL HINT: Take a breath, you're on your way to salvation.

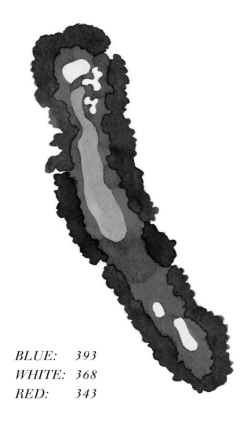

BLUE: 393
WHITE: 368
RED: 343

No.14　417 YARDS　PAR 4

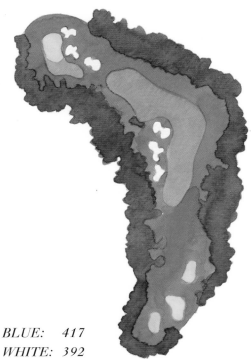

BLUE:　417
WHITE:　392
RED:　　360

Another severe dogleg; this time to the left. The designers had many options on how this and the next two holes would emerge. The version chosen dictated this extreme dogleg, with the fairway dropping away from the left. At the corner are three sand traps that are separate but in line with a tee shot. The good players will play a draw over the traps and the average player has plenty of room to the right. The size of the green has to be considered on the tee, since there is a tremendous advantage to being close. The green is relatively small, well above your head, and has a series of bunkers that interfere with a shot, especially if you are on the left side. This is one of the more difficult holes for the average player, since there is such an advantage to the player who can draw the ball accurately around the corner. The brush at the corner has been cleared fairly well, so that a shot that catches the top of the trees still has a chance, albeit a small one. The green has an opening at the front and is relatively easy to putt. No large undulations here, just a gentle slope towards the back.

HELPFUL HINT: When in doubt, punt. Oops, wrong sport.

No.15   210 YARDS   PAR 3

*T*his is a long par three. More often than not into the prevailing wind. But it is a little downhill. The inspiration for this hole was taken from the fifteenth at North Berwick, in Scotland. North Berwick is just a few miles east of Edinburgh, very close to the town of Gullan and the Muirfield Golf Club and within a couple hours drive of St. Andrews. Very nice company. The green sits at an angle to the tee box and is fronted by an area that will allow a ball to land short and with a fortuitous bounce wind up on the green. The dominant feature of the green, though, is this gigantic bunker that is as long as the green, situated on a parallel axis to the green, but closer to the tee than is the front of the green. From the tee, that is all your eyes and brain can absorb. It's definitely time to take pause and search for the reason you are here. If you're not in a tournament, you're here to enjoy yourself, so relax and make as good a swing as your tired body is up for. The green is peanut shaped with some undulations.

HELPFUL HINT: Par threes, one more to come.

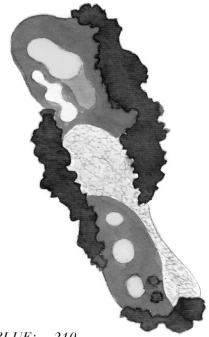

BLUE: 210
WHITE: 175
RED: 148

No. 16   439 YARDS   PAR 4

*T*his is the longest par four on the course. From the back tees, you have to carry the ball in the air for the first one hundred and fifty yards approximately in order to clear a ravine that runs across the fairway. For good players this wasteland does not pose any real problem, but for the average player it can be quite intimidating. There is a trap at the crux of the dogleg, but its main purpose is to give the player a focal point. It really does make it easier on the tee when you have a distinct target. The ideal shot is along the left side, not worrying about whether to carry the trap or not. Should you catch the bunker, well, *c'est la vie*. The hole, in its sweep to the right, follows the natural contours of the property, which flattens out as you get closer to the green. The green has an opening, if only a small one, and is protected by two substantial bunkers in the front. The back has a steep bank rising up to protect balls hit too far from reaching the road. Even though this bank is steep, it usually will not allow balls to roll back down to the green. Very awkward chips will result. From the very top of this bank your lie is good, but the green rolls away.

HELPFUL HINT: Birdie, you say?

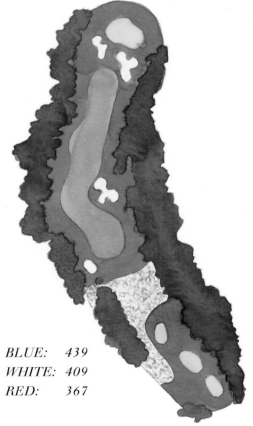

BLUE: 439
WHITE: 409
RED: 367

No. 17   163 YARDS   PAR 3

A short walk across the road, down a narrow path and there it is. This hole has an absolutely gorgeous natural setting. From the tee, to the right is a ravine, which is a water hazard. Filling this fairly deep ravine is heavy vegetation and some very tall, mature trees. It seems that the soil and the way water runs into the ravines is very conducive to good tree growth. The smaller pines were in the area that is now the fairway. The ravine continues behind the green. Both behind the green and to the right of the fairway is definitely lost ball territory. Since the player can determine the placement of the ball, and pick his personal favorite strategic position in the tee box, it is assumed that he will have a very good chance to wind up on the green. That's where the designers make the players earn their scores with the placement of traps for errant shots, and in creating areas on the green where the flagsticks might be placed. Some easy, most not. This green has two traps in front, the one on the left a smallish pot bunker that is not visible from the tee. Two bunkers behind, that actually will save your ball from running down the ravine into the brush.

HELPFUL HINT: With steady nerves you'll pull it off.

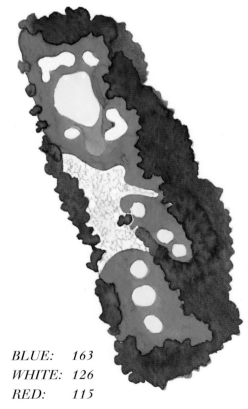

BLUE: 163
WHITE: 126
RED: 115

No. 18   500 YARDS   PAR 5

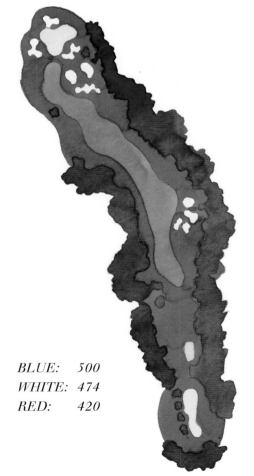

*T*he finishing hole is a well-designed par five with a dogleg to the left off the tee. A good finishing hole, especially for tournament play, ought to give a player the chance to improve his standing against the competition. A reward to a player who takes a chance and prevails. This par five offers that opportunity. From the tee the ball will have to travel a minimum of 220 yards to clear the corner. On the right are four traps. Further to the right at that point is deep grass with tall trees beyond that. Not a place that will be recalled fondly. Unfortunately slicers have gathered here since before the course actually opened for play. Up ahead, for the second shot, the ball needs to be on the left side, as far ahead as possible even though it becomes more difficult. The right side about thirty yards from the green has yet more sand traps circling a very tall Monterey Pine that will almost certainly deflect your ball further right should it come toward it. The green has three more bunkers spaced equally around the perimeter. Pin positions can be chosen on three levels. Putting from the wrong level produces some very interesting reads.

HELPFUL HINT: Are your buddies watching you from above?

BLUE: 500
WHITE: 474
RED: 420

THE TOURNAMENTS

*T*here is golf — the game you play with your friends as recreation. A welcome break from the world that usually dominates your time. The game of light-hearted bantering, being with friends, uniting against a common foe and hitting the occasional good shot. And then there is the crowning touch to a game that is already near perfect. Tournament play. This is a world of no excuses, a world where your last effort was indeed as good as you actually are and where your opposition is always treated with respect. There is no other sport where competitors shake each others' hands and sincerely wish each other the best of luck before the competition begins and then freely applaud extraordinary efforts. Great is expected.

The tournament player learns early to accept without debate all that is offered. Downhill, sidehill lies in the middle of the fairway, are accepted without reservation, not because it's just plain bad luck, but because that is the very essence of what golf is. In fact, on linksland courses where undulations in the fairways are commonplace, these contour changes are what players might consider the spice to an already well-seasoned meal. And once having tasted it, never to be done without again.

Much has been said about the camaraderie that exists between golfing competitors. The sharing of the good as well as the bad luck in the face of the inevitable. Because as surely as night follows day, the player will, having played in an inspired fashion, become a fumbling beginner. Jim Furyk, playing in the Memorial Tournament just a couple of strokes off the lead, found himself in a bunker about fifteen feet from the flagstick. In his own words, he says: "The reason I didn't get the ball out of the trap on my first attempt was that I was trying to be too cute. I just wanted to clear the top of the trap by an inch or so." Well, it took him three more shots after that to get out, which, as might be expected, put him out of contention. Honour and respect among competitors and for the game is alive and well. The rules are few, and are seldom black and white. They are written mostly in a loose, yet very precise fashion to be applied to individual and quite different locations. The touring pro will always solicit the opinion of his playing partner, as well as a tour official — just to be sure — when it comes to interpretations that are slightly out of the ordinary. Rules are enforced with consequences as severe as can be imagined, should they have been misinterpreted. For instance, signing a wrong score card — even if the mistake is not in your favor — may result in disqualification. Well, not too much pressure at this level of the game. One year, Craig Stadler, playing in the Buick Invitational in San Diego, drove his ball under a small tree. The lowest branches were about two feet off the ground, allowing the ball to be swiped at, if Craig could get low enough. He knelt down, on the moist but firm ground, and in order not to get his trousers dirty, placed a towel on the ground. No one present on either side of the ropes at the twelfth hole at Torrey Pines Golf Course thought anything of it. Craig at the time was two strokes ahead, and seemed destined to win, when a viewer called in and alerted the tournament committee to the fact that Mr. Stadler had improved his stance. Rule 13-3 says: "A player is entitled to place his feet firmly in taking his stance, but he shall not build a stance." Craig did not win the tournament and did not argue. Such is golf.

The Northern California Golf Association's primary function is to provide handicapping services to its members, then enabling players to enter competitions that are well organized. To this end the Rules and Competition Division works with two committees: Rules and Tournament. The Rules Committee determines the Rules of Play, Local Rules and Conditions of Competition that govern all NCGA tournament play. The Tournament Committee develops tournament policy, entry procedures, fees and eligibility, site and date of competition, and establishes a tournament program. The Tournament Committee organizes and conducts inter-club team match competitions. These three committees oversee a program which is multi-faceted and includes not only those events which the

Association conducts for its membership, but those which are conducted in conjunction with other organizations as well. Following is a brief description of the tournaments hosted by the NCGA and played at Spyglass Hill, Poppy Hills and Poppy Ridge which is the second course the NCGA commissioned. Poppy Ridge is near Livermore, a little north and east of the Monterey Peninsula. Incidentally, Poppy Ridge was designed by Rees Jones, Bobby's younger brother.

The Amateur. This is the oldest championship conducted by the NCGA. Started in 1906, this competition crowns the best amateur player. This event is for players with a handicap index of 4.4 or less. Approximately one hundred players after qualifying compete over 36 holes of stroke play. Thirty-two advance to single elimination match play, to determine the champion.

Four-Ball Competition. This event is for players with a handicap index of 5.4 or less. This championship begins with 18 holes of qualifying four-ball stroke play. The top sixty teams and ties advance to the

actual tournament, which is over 54 holes, with the field cut to forty teams after 36 holes.

Public Links Championship. This event is for players with a handicap index of 4.4 or less. There are two handicap flights, Presidents and Directors, for players with handicap indexes of 4.5 to 36.4 (to 40.4 for women). Entrants may not hold memberships at any course from which the general public is excluded. Contestants play 18 holes of qualifying stroke play, with 40 championship qualifiers and eighty handicap players advancing to the Championship Proper of 36 holes of stroke play.

Net Amateur Championship. This is a tournament for all, no matter what the index level. The format is a progressive-qualifying event starting with club competition to sectional qualifying with 120 contestants competing over 36 holes.

Senior Championship. This event is limited to players 55 years of age or older with a handicap index of 6.4 or less. The 120-man field plays 36 holes of stroke play over two days.

Senior Net Championship. This event is limited to players 55 years of age or older with a handicap index of 6.5 to 36.4. Players compete over 18 holes of qualifying in three flights determined by index. Forty players from each flight compete in the championship of 36 holes of stroke play over two days.

Master Stroke Play Championship. This event is limited to players between the ages of 40 to 54 with a handicap index of 5.4 or less. The previous years' champions and top ten performers and ties are exempt. A 128-man field plays 36 holes of stroke play over two days.

Junior Championship. This event is open to boys between 12 and 17 and girls between 15 and 17. The format is stroke play with boys between the ages of 14 and 17 playing 54 holes; 36 holes on Monday with the field cut for Tuesday's final 18 holes. Boys aged 12 to 13 and girls aged 15 to 17 play 18 holes per day, with no cut.

The NCGA joins other associations for tournaments such as: the San Joaquin/Sacramento Valley

Amateur, 14 Zone Competitions and the Associate Club Championship, the Four-Ball Net Championship, the Associate Club Four-Ball Net Championship, Parent/Junior, and the Team Match Competition. If that weren't enough the NCGA also co-administers qualifying tournaments for the California Golf Association, for the U.S. Open (local and sectional), the U.S. Senior Open, the U.S. Amateur and the U.S. Mid-Amateur. Not to be forgotten, the NCGA/CIF High School Championships and the Northern California Community College Championships. Quite a long list, that allows almost all who want to compete to do so with proper, professional administration.

And then, of course, there is the tournament for the professionals. Once a year, since 1985 when Cypress Point opted out of the rotation, for three days the pros and their mostly celebrity golfing partners come to Poppy Hills to compete in the AT&T Pebble Beach National Pro Am, formerly "The Crosby." The format for this tournament is: for the pros to be good enough, and for the amateurs to be well-connected and affluent enough. More specifically, each professional is assigned an amateur partner and as a team they play each of the three courses — Pebble Beach Golf Links, Spyglass Hill Golf Course and Poppy Hills Golf Course. After three rounds the field is cut to the low sixty professionals and the low twenty-five pro/am teams. Pebble Beach Golf Links is the venue for the closing round. This tournament is the only event on the professional tour where the amateur partners play on the final day. Making the cut and playing on Sunday is a lifelong dream for most amateurs. Jack Lemmon who has hardly missed a tournament in the last two decades, has not played on the final day, but will try again. And again.

This competition is quite different from the amateurs', carrying their own bags and bringing their own lunch. It does serve, though, to round out an extremely well-run tournament program which is alive and well at Poppy Hills Golf Course, high above all the other courses crowding the seashore below.

SOME GOLFERS WATCHING THEIR BALL IN FLIGHT

BRAD FAXON   NAME: — DATE: JAN. 1995

1	2	3	4	5	6	7	8	9	10	11	12	13	14	15	16	17	18	
413	162	406	560	426	181	388	390	557	511	214	531	393	417	210	439	163	500	6861
3	3	3	4	3	3	3	3	5	4	3	4	4	3	4	5	3	4	64
4	3	4	5	4	3	4	4	5	5	3	5	4	4	3	4	3	5	72

BRAD FAXON'S COURSE RECORD SETTING ROUND

*T*he day was by all accounts ordinary. It had rained, quite hard on the previous days, but on this Friday the second day of the AT&T Pebble Beach National Pro-Am, the skies were clear and the temperature was around 82 degrees Fahrenheit. But then, Brad birdied the first, sinking a 25 foot putt. Well, this was not out of the ordinary, since he is one of the very best putters on the professional tour. Then he went on to birdie three, four and five, seven and eight, with a par at six and finished the front nine with a par at nine. Now, all who watched, including Brad, had an idea that this day might not be ordinary after all. The back nine seemed to be much the same as the front, since he started with birdies on ten, twelve and fourteen with two pars mixed in. Then unfortunately two bogeys on fourteen and fifteen, with a birdie on eighteen that almost was an eagle. This 64 is the lowest round since the course opened for play. It must be noted that on that day winter rules were in effect, allowing the players to lift clean and place. Tom Watson, playing the course the same day, said it might have been a two stroke difference. But, lets not rain on Brad's parade, after all the temperature was 82 degrees in the shade and the skies were clear.

DEER ON THE FIRST TEE — WITHOUT SPIKES, CLUBS, OR SCORECARDS

THE GOWAN CYPRESS

ACKNOWLEDGMENTS

Mother Nature has to be thanked for the immense beauty She bestowed on the Monterey Peninsula.

Bobby Jones Jr. has to be thanked for not abusing Her creation, but enhancing its beauty.

The NCGA has to be thanked for being a more than capable organization, resulting in the need for a golf course.

All help given is significant, even when at first glance seemingly unimportant.

A special thanks to Kevin Orona who helped and encouraged me at the outset.

Paul Porter who granted the necessary permissions, Don Knott who gave his expertise readily, along with

Bob Higgins the Director of Golf at Poppy Hills Golf Course, John Zoller for insights into the NCGA,

Roger Val for his expertise, Cathy Schertzer and her charming staff,

and finally, Jim Donoahue a man who helped me and was my mentor for many years.

And to Tony Roberts, Susan Kuchinskas, Steve and Noel Machat.

Again, to all, a very sincere thank you.

ALL PHOTOGRAPHS ©1998 UDO MACHAT, SPORT IMAGES

STEVE